Let's Get Active™

LET'S PLAY

BASEBALL

Shane McFee

PowerKiDS press™

New York

Published in 2008 by The Rosen Publishing Group, Inc.
29 East 21st Street, New York, NY 10010

First Edition

Editor: Jennifer Way and Nicole Pristash
Book Design: Greg Tucker
Photo Researcher: Nicole Pristash

Photo Credits: Cover, pp. 5, 13 Shutterstock.com; pp. 7, 21 © Getty Images; p. 9 © www.iStockphoto.com/Rob Friedman; p. 11 © www.iStockphoto.com/Ronald Manera; p. 15 © www.iStockphoto.com; p. 17 © www.iStockphoto.com/James Boulette; p. 19 © Ken Chernus/Getty Images.

Library of Congress Cataloging-in-Publication Data

McFee, Shane.
  Let's play baseball / by Shane McFee. — 1st ed.
      p. cm. — (Let's get active)
  Includes index.
  ISBN 978-1-4042-4194-7 (library binding)
  1. Baseball—United States—Juvenile literature. I. Title.
  GV867.5M4 2008
  796.357—dc22
                                        2007034648

Manufactured in the United States of America

Contents

National Pastime

Have you ever played baseball? Baseball is one of the most common sports that kids play in the United States. Many Americans watch baseball games at ballparks and on television. Baseball is often called the national **pastime**. This is because baseball was first played in the United States. The first American sports superstars were baseball players.

Baseball can be hard to learn at first. With practice, however, you can learn all the rules and have a lot of fun!

Many kids play baseball on a team at school or in their town, like this player.

Bat-and-Ball

Baseball has been around for over 200 years. It is played by hitting a ball with a piece of wood, called a bat. Baseball began when Irish and British **immigrants** brought an old game called bat-and-ball to the United States. Bat-and-ball was also called rounders. There were many different forms of bat-and-ball. Over the years, these games evolved, or changed, into baseball and the game we know today.

Today, baseball is one of the biggest sports in the world. It is played in the United States and many other countries, such as Canada, Mexico, and Japan.

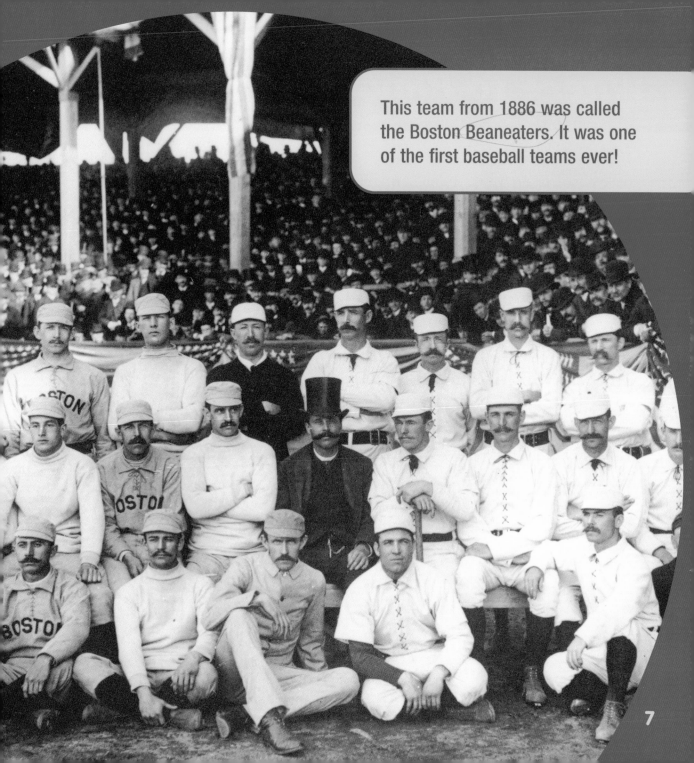

This team from 1886 was called the Boston Beaneaters. It was one of the first baseball teams ever!

Baseball is generally played on a baseball field. A baseball field has two parts. The infield is shaped like a **diamond**. Each point of the diamond has a base, on which players step. The four bases are called home plate, first base, second base, and third base. The rest of the field is called the outfield.

To play a game of baseball, you need a baseball, a bat, and a **glove**. Right-handed people wear a baseball glove on their left hand. Left-handed people wear it on their right hand.

Baseball players wear baseball hats. This player's hat is keeping the sun out of his eyes so he can see the baseball.

Play Ball!

Two teams play a game of baseball. Each team has nine players playing at one time. One team plays **offense**, by scoring runs, or points, by hitting the ball and running around the bases. This is called batting. A run is scored when an offensive player reaches home plate. The other team plays **defense** when it is out in the field. The team tries to stop the batters on the other team from getting on base and scoring at home plate.

A baseball game lasts for nine innings. An inning is the amount of time it takes for both teams to take one turn batting and one turn fielding.

This batter is holding on to the bat with both hands. He also has his feet spread apart and has one knee bent. This position will help him hit the ball.

11

Strike Three! You're Out!

When a batter hits the ball, he runs to first base. The runner tries to reach the next base in order to score a run at home plate. It is up to the defensive team to keep him from scoring, by getting the player out.

An out happens when the defensive team tags, or touches, the base that the runner is running to or the runner himself. An out also happens when the defensive team catches the ball that the batter hit. If the batter swings and misses, he gets a strike. Three strikes make one out. Once the fielding team gets three outs, it is their turn to come up to bat.

A pitcher has to wind up before throwing the baseball. This is so he can throw the ball hard enough to strike out the batter.

The Players

There are many positions on a baseball team. The pitcher is the most important because he has to pitch the ball past the batter. The catcher bends down behind home plate and catches the pitches. The players at first, second, and third base guard their base. They also throw and catch the ball with the others players. The shortstop stands between second and third base. Shortstops must be in good shape. Most batters hit the ball right at them!

There are three players in the outfield. They must have strong arms so they can throw the ball into the infield.

The catcher is in a dangerous place and can be hit by the baseball. To keep himself safe, he wears a mask and special pads.

The Lineup

Like most sports teams, baseball teams have **coaches**. In baseball, they are called managers. A manager plans the team's **strategy**.

The manager also decides the team's lineup. The lineup is the order in which the players come up to bat. It is very important to have a good lineup. The first batter should be a good hitter and a fast runner. The second batter should also be a good hitter so that she can advance the first batter around the bases. The third batter is generally the best hitter on the team. She must be able to advance the first and second batters so they can score. Baseball players help each other.

Sometimes a batter will drop his body to the ground in order to reach the base faster. This is called a slide.

Teamwork

Playing baseball is a great way to have fun and to exercise. It also teaches you teamwork. Teamwork means working together with others. Baseball players have to work together in order to win. The first baseman has to trust the shortstop to make a good throw. The pitcher has to trust the catcher to catch the ball.

Baseball also teaches you how to be a good sport. This means being a good loser and a good winner. Baseball players must be respectful to each other. This is what it takes to be a good baseball player.

These baseball players are cheering for their teammate. This is a great way to practice teamwork.

Meet David Ortiz

David Ortiz is the **designated** hitter for the Boston Red Sox. In the American League, pitchers do not have to bat in the lineup. The designated hitter bats for the pitcher. Ortiz is one of the best hitters in Major League Baseball.

Ortiz was born in the Dominican Republic. He came to the United States to play **professional** baseball when he was only 17. He holds his team's record for the most home runs in a season. A home run is when a player hits the ball behind the fence in the outfield. The player gets to run around the bases and score at home plate. In 2006, Ortiz hit 54 home runs!

In his first 10 years of playing professional baseball, David Ortiz hit more than 250 home runs!

Let's Get Active!

Do you want to learn how to play baseball? You can start by playing a game of catch. Catch is when two people throw the ball to each other. It is a great way to learn catching and throwing. These skills are not as easy to learn as they sound. You will need to practice them.

You can also play on a team by **joining** Little League Baseball. Little League Baseball is made up of many teams across the country. There are likely some in your area. You can find out more about baseball teams on the Internet or at the library. Have fun and play ball!

Glossary

coaches (KOHCH-ez) People who direct a team.

defense (DEE-fents) When a team tries to stop the other team from scoring.

designated (DEH-zig-nayt-ed) Picked for a special task.

diamond (DY-uh-mund) A shape with four sides.

glove (GLUV) A covering for the hand made with a space for each finger and for the thumb.

immigrants (IH-muh-grunts) People who move to a new country from another country.

joining (JOYN-ing) Coming together or taking part in.

offense (AH-fents) When a team tries to score points in a game.

pastime (PAS-tym) An activity that makes time pass in an enjoyable way.

professional (pruh-FESH-nul) Someone who is paid for what he or she does.

strategy (STRA-tuh-jee) Planning and directing different plays in team sports.

Index

Web Sites

Due to the changing nature of Internet links, PowerKids Press has developed an online list of Web sites related to the subject of this book. This site is updated regularly. Please use this link to access the list:

www.powerkidslinks.com/lga/base/